4 Carpets should be fastened down properly, especially on stairs

5 Stairs should be well lit. If you have steps outside, they too should be lit

6 Is your hot water supply thermostatically controlled to avoid scalding water?

7 Your water pipes should be lagged to prevent bursts in winter

8 Are all medicines fitted with childproof caps, and kept together out of children's reach?

9 Are all disinfectants, bleach, detergents, pesticides etc. clearly marked and stored where children cannot reach them?

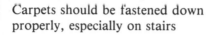

First edition

© LADYBIRD BOOKS LTD MCMLXXXI

Home Safety

by
MARJORY PURVES Dip C O T

with illustrations by
CAROLE HUGHES
and 'Simla' cartoon drawings by
KEITH LOGAN

Ladybird Books Loughborough

My name is Sam

and this is my friend
Simla.

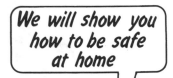

*We will show you
how to be safe
at home*

4

I live with my Mum and Dad
and my baby sister Jane.

Our house
has an upstairs

and a downstairs.

Do you have stairs?
Are the stairs inside the house?
Are the stairs outside the house?

Our stairs are
inside the house.
We have a gate
at the top of
the stairs. Now
Jane cannot fall
downstairs.

I come down
one step at a time.

Shut the gate carefully
and hold the rail

Mums and Dads

*Make sure that your stairs are
well lit, and that the carpet is
not loose or worn.
Show your child how to use the
stairs safely.
A safety gate, made to BS4125,
should be used at the top and
bottom of the stairs.*

My friend has stairs
outside her home.
Her home is high up
on the seventh floor.

Never climb on the
balcony! It's a long
way down to the road

Mums and Dads

It is easy not to notice your child climbing, if you are talking to a neighbour. Keep your child in front of you where you can see him.

7

Is there a LIFT
outside your home?
The lift goes up
and down.
It carries people
and prams
and shopping bags.

Stop! Let Mum or Dad
help you to press the
button to open the
lift door

Play this rhyming game.

Tall
shop
in
the
town

Lifts
moving up
and down

Mums and Dads
A child can cause a lift to break down or stop between floors by playing with the controls.

Warn him of the dangers to himself and other people.

Doors swinging round about

People moving in and out.

In big shops, Dad helps me to step on to the escalator and and I hold the rail. I know I must stay within the yellow lines.

Mums and Dads

If you are using an escalator, lift your child on and off.

Pushchairs should not be wheeled on to an escalator.

Do you like to climb?
I like to climb.

I can climb on the slide at Playschool.
I can climb on the frame in the park
if Mum is near me.

Mums and Dads

Children need the adventure of climbing and jumping as part of growing up.
Stand near your child to watch, *but don't help him to climb. He knows himself how far he can go without difficulty.*

I can climb on tree stumps in the woods.
But I MUST NOT CLIMB on chairs
to reach up high.

Be safe! Ask a grown up to reach for you

Mums and Dads

Try to have the things that you use every day within easy reach. Do not let your child see you climb on a chair to reach high shelves. Children like to copy adults.
Use household steps for safety.

Do you have a baby at home?
Jane is our baby. She is growing big.

When babies are little,
they cry, and they smile,
and they sleep.

Mums have to feed them,
wash them, dress them
and carry them.

Mums and Dads

Hold a bottle-fed baby in your arms while he or she is feeding. Never prop the bottle up for a baby to feed alone.

Do not give a baby a soft pillow in the pram or cot, and use a cat net on the pram if the baby is sleeping outside.

When babies grow
bigger, they try
to climb like me.

Babies seem to have long arms,
and they throw things.

Mums and Dads

If you use a tablecloth, secure the folds at each corner with a clothes peg. Use unbreakable dishes for baby's food, and make sure that the high-chair is well away from the table and teapot.

When babies grow bigger,
they crawl very quickly.

When you know how to
be safe help Mum
to keep the baby safe

Babies put things
into their mouths.
I keep my toys
away from Jane.
Some of them are
small and hard.
Jane could choke
on them, or
swallow them.

Mums and Dads

*Stay with the baby who is
starting to crawl and walk.
If you have to leave the room,
put him into the playpen or the
cot to play, or into a baby chair,*
*where he is safe.
Do not expect an older child to
look after the baby too often.
This causes resentment and
leads to accidents.*

14

I give Jane her own toys to play with.

Simla has a
guessing game on
the next page. Can
you play it with us?

Mums and Dads
Throw out any plastic toys that split.
Check that the eyes in soft toys are securely fixed before you buy them, whether new or secondhand.

A GUESSING GAME

Mums and Dads
Play this game with your child, or put some soft and some sharp things on a tray and let him guess.

16

Look at the pictures.

Which things are sharp ?

Sharp things can cut your fingers.

answers on page 50

Do not play with sharp or broken things. They can hurt you

Dad says that my toys are
everywhere.
Can you count the number of toys
that I have left on the floor?
Someone could cut himself
if he fell over my cars.
Have a look round your home.
Are there other things that can
be tripped over?

Do you have a box for your toys?
Dad is going to help me to make one.

Making a Toy Box

You will need:

A strong cardboard box
from the grocer

Two pieces of old clothes
rope or thick string for
handles

Some flour and water
mixed to a paste

An old paint brush to
spread the paste

Blunt-nosed scissors

Old magazines

Cut out some bright pictures.
Paste them on to the sides of the box.
Ask Dad or Mum to make two holes
at each end of the box.
To make each handle, push the ends
of the piece of rope through the holes.
Tie a knot at each end of the handles.

Fire can hurt you!
It is very hot
and can burn you.
It can burn your house

Now I have put my toys into the new box. Simla is looking at the fireplace. A piece of coal has fallen out of the fire.

Mums and Dads
The best fireguard is the nursery guard BS3140.
It should have side clips that fit into permanent wall fastenings.

Guard all fires – electric, gas, coal or paraffin, with sparkguards where necessary.

NEVER play with fire.
NEVER poke pieces of paper into the fire.
Fire can HURT you.
It will BURN you.

It's a good job Mum remembered to put the fireguard round the fire

Mums and Dads

Never dry washing over a fireguard or convector heater. Do not let children see you lighting a paper taper from the fire.

Fill paraffin heaters, and change gas cylinders, outside. Put them where they cannot be knocked over and never move heaters when lit.

Have you seen firemen putting out a fire in a house?

There is a lot of black smoke and flames. The people who live in the house are safe now, but everything is wet with the water from the hoses. Everything is dirty from the smoke.

NEVER play with fire

Can you draw or paint a picture of a
fire engine?
Here is my picture of a fire engine.
Listen to the sound of the fire engine
as it goes by. It is very loud.
Can you make that sound?

Mums and Dads

*If there is a fire station near you,
show your children the fire
engines. Show them the fire
escapes on big buildings, and
the water hydrant squares on*
*the pavement.
Encourage your child to go to
the window to see and hear
fire engines passing.*

Can you think of other things in your house that become hot?

We need heat . . .

. . . to cook our food.

We need heat . . .

. . . to give us light.

. . . to boil water.

We need heat . . .

. . . to wash clothes

. . . to iron Dad's shirt.

. . . to keep us warm.

How do all these things become hot?
The wires carrying electricity are
under the floor and behind the walls.

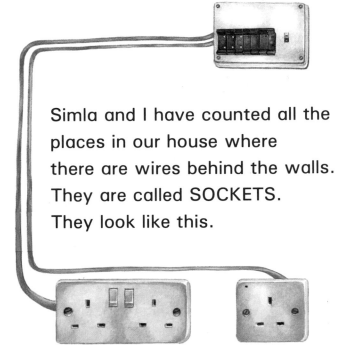

Simla and I have counted all the
places in our house where
there are wires behind the walls.
They are called SOCKETS.
They look like this.

Mums and Dads

*Fit safety socket covers, if
possible, when the sockets are
not in use.
Make sure that plugs are wired
properly.*

*If the plugs have fuses inside,
check that the fuse is the
correct one for the appliance
used.
Here is a list to help you.*

Have you counted the number of
sockets in your house?
Count them with Mum or Dad.

When you are
counting, look with
your eyes.
DO NOT TOUCH
THE SOCKETS.

3 Amp	5 Amp	13 Amp
Blanket	Drill (up to 1,000 watts)	Drill (1,000 watts plus)
Clock	Iron	Fire
Coffee Percolator	Toaster	Kettle
Drill (750 watts or under)	Sewing Machine	Refrigerator
Lamp		Spindryer
Mixer		Vacuum Cleaner
Radio	1 Amp	Washing Machine
Record Player		Lawn Mower
Tape Recorder	Shaver Socket	Freezer
Television Set		

Watch Mum cooking the dinner.
She turns the handles of the pans
to the back of the cooker.
She puts on the pan lids
very carefully.

The pans are very hot.
The cooker is hot all over.

When the water in the pan becomes very hot, it turns to steam.

Look at the steam. It is very hot. It is very strong. It pushes the pan lids up and down. Steam is very hot. It can scald you.

Boiling water can scald!

Mums and Dads

A Fire Blanket is recommended for the kitchen. A safety guard can be bought for the cooker (your local Gas or Electricity Board will have details). Keep children away from the cooker, and explain to them why.
A flint lighter for a gas cooker is safer than matches. If deep-frying, use a pan that covers the boiling ring. Do not fill it more than one-third full, and do not use a lid. Never leave a chip pan unattended, and do not let it overheat. Dry the chips well, and take extra care when frying frozen foods.
Children can be severely burned by boiling fat or oil.

Mum is making
jam tarts and cakes
today.
I am making things
with this pastry.
I can roll it,
and push it,
and pull it.

Now I have made a little man. Mum is
putting him into the oven. The oven is
very hot.

Mum wears a big,
thick glove on her
hand. The oven tray
gets very hot.

How to make playdough

You will need:

2 cupfuls of unsifted flour

1 cupful of salt

About one cupful of water

2 tablespoonfuls of melted cooking fat or oil

Mix everything together in a bowl. Then *knead* (press and pull) the mixture till it is like bread dough. Mum can add a little food colouring to the water to make different colours of playdough.

Hot or Cold?

Which of these things are HOT?

Did you guess that the tap is a hot tap?

We have a hot tap and a cold tap
on our washbasin.

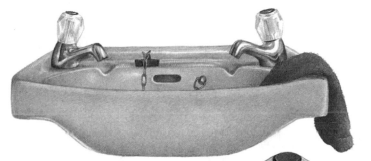

Do you have colours
on your taps?
Look and see!
Red for HOT.
Blue or Green for COLD.

Some taps have
HOT or COLD
marked on them.

Mums and Dads
Show your child the taps at your
kitchen sink and in the
bathroom.
If your immersion heater has a
variable thermostat, have it
adjusted so that the hot water is
never at scalding temperature.

Be SAFE in the bathroom.

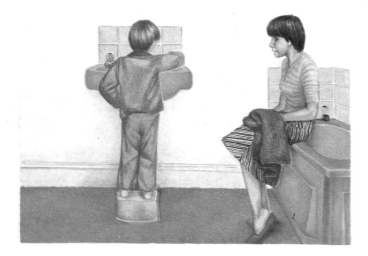

*First some cold water
then some hot water
and never fill
the basin too full*

Now the water is warm
on my hands, not too cold
and not too hot.

Mums and Dads

*Keep medicines and bathroom
cleaners in a locked cupboard,
out of the child's reach.*

*An inexpensive safety latch for
cupboards and drawers is
available from Babyboots.*

Turn off the taps carefully,
and don't forget to pull out the plug
when you have finished!

Mums and Dads

Watch over your child in the bathroom.
He or she may need a 'Grow-tall' step (Mothercare) to reach the washbasin, and a toilet trainer seat fitted over the adult one. Both of these will help him or her to become more independent. Fit an escape lock on your bathroom door. This can be unscrewed from the outside if the child locks the door on the inside.
Bathroom heaters should be high up on the wall. These and the light should have a pull-cord switch.

It is time for my
bath. I like to play
in the bath. Do you
play in the bath?
Mum puts a mat
in the bath so that
I will not slip. She
turns on the cold
tap first. Then she
turns on the hot tap.

*Wait until Mum tests
the water!
It may be too hot*

Make a Pouring Set for Playing in the Bath

Cut here and sandpaper edges

You will need:
An empty plastic squash bottle

Ask Mum or Dad to cut round the bottle with a pair of scissors.
Make the edges smooth with sandpaper.

Now you have a funnel and a mug for pouring.

Listen to the water pouring through the funnel.

Mums and Dads

Give your child a little time to play in the bath.
Water play is very soothing and
satisfying. He learns from it.
While pouring and measuring, he is learning to control his hands.

37

Simla and I
are playing a
Listening Game.

Will you play it
with us?
Shut your eyes.
Sit quietly.

Now listen to the sounds
outside the window.
What can YOU hear?
Can you hear a bus,
or a lorry?
Can you hear a car,
or a motorbike?

Mums and Dads
Listening makes a child aware of what is going on round about him.

If he is aware of danger, he can avoid it more easily.

Shut your eyes and listen to the sounds INSIDE the room.

What can you hear?
Can you hear a clock ticking,
or Mum talking?

Can you hear a
tap running,

or the fire crackling?

Listen carefully and be SAFE.
SAFE outside, because you can hear
the traffic coming.
SAFE inside, because you can hear
Mum and Dad if they call.

If you hear a new sound at home always ask what it is. Mum may not have heard it

39

Here is a song about Listening
and Looking.
Do you know it?

I hear thunder
I hear thunder
Oh don't you
Oh don't you.
Pitter, patter, raindrops
Pitter, patter, raindrops.
I'm wet through
I'm wet through.

I see blue skies
I see blue skies
Way up high
Way up high.
Hurry up the sunshine
Hurry up the sunshine
I'll soon dry
I'll soon dry.

Make a Traffic Scrapbook

You will need:
Blunt-nosed scissors
Old magazines or
  newspapers
Paste and a brush
A scrapbook (folded
  wallpaper will do).

Cut out pictures of all kinds of traffic.

Paste them into your scrapbook.

Can you find a
picture of a car,
or a bicycle,
or a motorbike?

A motorbike has
only two wheels,
but it moves very
fast.

Do you remember
listening to the
sound of a motorbike?

Mums and Dads
If your child cannot use scissors *him paste them.*
yet, cut out the pictures and let *Talk to him about the pictures.*

Sometimes I am noisy and rush about.
When I rush about I trip,

and I fall,

and I break things

Do not rush!

CAN YOU?

Can you walk on tiptoe,
As softly as a cat?
Can you stamp along the road?
Stamp! Stamp! Just like that.
Can you take some great big strides
Just like a giant can?
Or walk along so slowly
Like a poor old, bent old man?
Can you?

Simla and I walk on tiptoe to the garden shed.

Do you have a garden shed? It is just like a little house. Dad locks the door with a big padlock. Today the door is open. Dad is busy inside.

Look at the tools hanging on the wall.
Some of them are sharp.
Sharp things can cut your fingers.

The shed has a high shelf full of bottles and tins. I must not touch the shelf.

Digging has made us hot and dry.

Mum will give us some squash in a cup.

Mums and Dads

Keep poisons, household cleaners, disinfectants and paraffin locked away. Never put them into soft drink bottles, and make sure they are labelled clearly.
Warn your child when you are putting these things away.

Now look at this picture.
How many things can you
see that are NOT SAFE?

answers on page 50

47

It is bedtime.
We have had a busy day.
Jane is in her cot.
Mum pulls up the cot side
so that Jane will not climb out.

If I look out of the window,
I can see the moon.

Mums and Dads

Before buying a drop-side cot, ensure that it conforms to British Safety Standards.
Fit safety latches to windows and remember to lock them after cleaning the windows. Safety rails can also be fitted.
Keep chairs well away from windows – children climb.
Use an extra guard on all heaters.

Dad has come to tell me
a story. I like to look at
pictures.
I like to listen to stories.

Do you Look and Listen?

Mums and Dads

*Make bedtime a quiet time.
Accidents often happen at times
when children and parents are
overtired.
Look at picture books with your
child. Let him or her talk about
the pictures and unwind after*
*a busy day.
A safety bed barrier is available
(Babyboots) to reassure the child
when he or she first moves from
a cot to a bed, and to prevent
him or her falling out.*

Simla and I have shown you how to be SAFE at home all day.

Mum and Dad always make our home SAFE all night before they go to sleep.

ANSWERS TO PAGES 46 and 47
Mum on stool instead of proper steps
No fireguard around fire   Toys scattered on floor
Baby about to pull table cloth with teapot and candles
Candles burning on tree and mantelpiece
Cards on mantelpiece above fire   Mirror above fireplace
Stocking held by candle
Too many leads into one socket

ANSWERS TO PAGES 16 and 17
An open tin   A broken bottle   A knife
Pointed scissors   Pins   Dad's razor

51

BE SAFE
LAST THING AT NIGHT
**here are some things
you should ALWAYS do**

Switch all fires off. If you have an open fire, leave it guarded

Check that all water taps are turned off